Ethixtech Chronicles

# How to build games

*Dedication*

*To the Visionaries, Innovators, and Pixel Pioneers,*
*In the ever-evolving symphony of technology, you are the composers, weaving melodies of innovation and creativity. "GameCraft 101" is dedicated to you—those who dare to dream, code, and shape the future of gaming. Your passion and ingenuity inspire us all. May your games reach new heights and resonate across the digital cosmos.*

*With admiration and a shared commitment to ethical exploration.*

*Ethixtech Chronicles*

Epigraph by ETHIXTECH CHRONICLES:

"In the realm where code meets canvas, 'GameCraft 101' is a guiding light. As the EthixTech Chronicles, we celebrate the fusion of ethics and technology, applauding creators shaping digital narratives. May this book be your compass in the vast seas of creativity and possibility in game development."

ETHIXTECH CHRONICLES
Ethixtech                    Chronicles

# Contents



1.

2.

3.

4.

5.

6.

7.

8.

9.

10.

11.

12.

13.

14.

15.

16.

17.

# Foreword

Foreword by ETHIXTECH CHRONICLES:

In the ever-evolving tapestry of technology, gaming stands as a vibrant thread, weaving tales of innovation, passion, and boundless creativity. "GameCraft 101" emerges as a guiding star in this celestial realm, illuminating the path for both seasoned developers and aspiring visionaries.

As the EthixTech Chronicles, we've witnessed the transformative power of technology and the immense impact it has on shaping our digital narratives. "GameCraft 101" not only serves as a comprehensive manual for building games but also as a testament to the dedication and ingenuity required to thrive in the dynamic landscape of the Google Play Store.

In these pages, you'll find a trove of insights, expert advice, and a roadmap that transcends the technicalities of coding, offering a holistic approach to game development. The authors have masterfully blended technical know-how with the artistry of storytelling, creating a compelling guide that resonates with the very essence of game creation.

May this book be your compass in the vast seas of game development, navigating you through the challenges, igniting your creativity, and ultimately catapulting your creation onto the stage of the Google Play Store. The journey ahead is thrilling, and "GameCraft 101" is your trusted companion on this epic odyssey.

Happy crafting, and may your games leave an indelible mark on the digital cosmos!

ETHIXTECH                                    CHRONICLES

# Preface

Preface:

Welcome to the exciting world of game development and Google Play Store publishing! "GameCraft 101" is your passport to the realm of endless creativity, where the spark of an idea transforms into an immersive digital experience. In these pages, you'll embark on a journey that demystifies the art of game creation and unveils the secrets to launching your masterpiece on the Google Play Store.

This guide is not just about coding and design; it's a roadmap infused with the essence of passion and innovation. Whether you're a seasoned developer seeking new insights or a budding creator taking your first steps, "GameCraft 101" is crafted to be your companion, offering practical strategies, expert advice, and a treasure trove of tips to turn your dream game into a reality.

So, let's dive into the world of pixels, lines of code, and the boundless possibilities of game development. Your odyssey begins now, and the Play Store awaits your digital masterpiece!

# Acknowledgement

Acknowledgment by ETHIXTECH CHRONICLES:

In the dynamic world of technology and innovation, collaboration is the heartbeat that propels us forward. As the EthixTech Chronicles, we stand at the intersection of ethics and technology, witnessing the incredible impact creators have on shaping our digital landscape.

To the authors of "GameCraft 101," we extend our heartfelt appreciation. Your dedication to demystifying the art of game development and sharing invaluable insights reflects the spirit of collaboration that defines our industry. This book not only equips developers with the tools for success but also serves as a testament to the limitless possibilities when creativity meets technology.

We commend your commitment to empowering the next generation of game developers and enthusiasts. The EthixTech Chronicles proudly acknowledges the contributions of the authors and celebrates the vibrant community that continues to push the boundaries of what's possible.

May "GameCraft 101" inspire countless creators to embark on their own journeys, leaving an indelible mark on the canvas of the digital world.

ETHIXTECH                                    CHRONICLES

# 1

# Choose a Game Development Platform

Certainly! Let's delve deeper into the first step:

1. Choose a Game Development Platform:

Research and Exploration:Before diving into game development, it's crucial to choose a platform that aligns with your goals and skill level. Here are some key considerations:

a. Unity:

Description: Unity is a widely used, versatile game development platform suitable for both beginners and professionals.
    -Strengths:
    - User-friendly interface.

- Large community and extensive documentation.
- Cross-platform support (iOS, Android, PC, etc.).
- Asset Store for ready-made assets and tools.

b. Unreal Engine:D

Description: Unreal Engine is renowned for its powerful graphics and is often used for high-end games.
-Strengths:
- Stunning visuals and realistic graphics.
- Robust built-in tools for animation, cinematics, and physics.
- Suitable for both 2D and 3D games.

c. Godot:

Description: Godot is an open-source game engine, known for its simplicity and flexibility.
-Strengths:
- Lightweight and easy to learn.
- No licensing fees.
- Supports both 2D and 3D game development.

Consider Your Game Concept:
-Genre and Complexity:

- Consider the type of game you want to create (e.g., 2D platformer, 3D shooter, puzzle game).

- Assess the complexity of your game concept and choose a platform that aligns with those requirements.

Learning the Basics:

a. Unity:

-Documentation and Tutorials:

- Explore Unity's official documentation and tutorials available on their website.

- Online platforms like Unity Learn and YouTube offer extensive resources for beginners.

b. Unreal Engine:

- Official Learning Resources:

- Utilize Unreal Engine's official learning resources, including documentation and video tutorials.

- Unreal Engine's YouTube channel provides in-depth tutorials for various skill levels.

c. Godot:

-Documentation and Community:

- Refer to Godot's official documentation and community forums for guidance.

- The Godot Engine YouTube channel offers video tutorials for practical learning.

Hands-On Practice:

a. Unity:

- Create a Simple Project:

- Start with a basic project to understand Unity's interface.

- Experiment with adding objects, applying materials, and implementing simple scripts.

b. Unreal Engine:

-Explore Blueprints:

- Learn the basics of Blueprints, Unreal Engine's visual scripting system.

- Create a simple game mechanic to get hands-on experience.

c. Godot:

- Node System:

- Understand Godot's node system for scene building.

- Create a simple game prototype to grasp the fundamentals.

Conclusion:

Choosing the right game development platform is a pivotal decision that sets the foundation for your game creation journey.

Take the time to explore each platform, consider your game concept, and immerse yourself in learning the basics through documentation, tutorials, and hands-on practice. Remember, the chosen platform should align with your project's requirements and your personal preferences as a developer.

# 2

# Learn the Basics of Your Chosen Game Development Platform

2. Learn the Basics of Your Chosen Game Development Platform:

Once you've chosen a game development platform, it's essential to familiarize yourself with its core features, tools, and programming languages. Let's delve into the process of learning the basics:

Unity:

1. Unity Interface:

Explore the Unity Editor's interface, including the Scene view, Game view, Hierarchy, and Project panes.

Understand the components of a Unity project, such as scenes, assets, and prefabs.

2. Unity Scripting (C#):

Learn the basics of C#, Unity's primary scripting language.

Understand variables, functions, and control flow structures.

Practice writing simple scripts to manipulate game objects.

3. Game Objects and Components:

Grasp the concept of GameObjects and Components in Unity.

Understand how to create, manipulate, and organize game objects using the Inspector.

4. Physics and Colliders:

Explore Unity's physics system and understand concepts like rigidbodies, colliders, and joints.

Implement basic interactions using Unity's built-in physics engine.

5. Animation:

Learn how to create animations using Unity's Animator.

Understand the process of rigging and animating characters or objects.

6. UI Design:

Explore Unity's UI system for creating user interfaces.

Learn how to design menus, buttons, and interactive elements.

Unreal Engine:

1. Unreal Engine Interface:

Familiarize yourself with the Unreal Editor, including the Viewport, Content Browser, and Details panel.

Understand the structure of a typical Unreal Engine project.

2. Blueprint Visual Scripting:

Learn the basics of Blueprint visual scripting.

Understand nodes, variables, and events in the visual scripting system.

3. Materials and Shaders:

Explore Unreal Engine's material editor.

Understand how to create and apply materials and shaders to objects.

4. Level Design:

Learn the fundamentals of level design in Unreal Engine.

Use landscape tools and create basic environments.

5.Animation and Sequencer:

Understand the animation system in Unreal Engine, including Persona for character animation.

Explore the Sequencer for cinematic and in-game sequences.

6. Particle Systems:

Learn how to create and customize particle systems for special effects.

Godot:

1. Godot Interface:

Explore the Godot Editor, including the Scene, Inspector, and FileSystem panes.

Understand scenes and the node system.

2. GDScript Programming:

Learn GDScript, Godot's scripting language.

Understand variables, functions, and control structures.

3. Node System:

Grasp the concept of nodes and scenes in Godot.

Understand how to create and organize scenes using the node system.

4.2D and 3D Game Development:

Depending on your project, explore either 2D or 3D game development in Godot.

Understand the differences in the workflow for each.

5. Physics and Collision:

Learn how to implement physics and collision detection in Godot.

Experiment with rigidbodies and collision shapes.

General Tips:

Official Documentation:

Refer to the official documentation of your chosen platform regularly.

Documentation serves as a comprehensive guide to features, functions, and best practices.

Online Tutorials:

Explore online tutorials on platforms like Unity Learn, Unreal Engine's official YouTube channel, and Godot Engine's tutorials.

Follow step-by-step guides to reinforce your understanding.

Community Engagement:

Join forums, communities, and social media groups related to your chosen platform.

Engage with other developers, ask questions, and share your progress.

Project-Based Learning:

Apply your knowledge by working on small projects.

Start with simple games to practice and gradually increase complexity.

By thoroughly understanding the basics of your chosen game development platform, you'll lay a solid foundation for creating engaging and functional games. Remember, continuous learning and hands-on experience are key to mastering game development.

# 3

# Design Your Game

3. Design Your Game:

Designing your game is a crucial phase that sets the creative and conceptual direction for your project. Here's an extensive guide to help you navigate the process:

Conceptualize Your Game:

1. Define Your Game Concept:

Clearly articulate the core idea of your game. What is the genre? What makes it unique?

Consider the target audience and tailor your concept accordingly.

2. Create a Game Design Document (GDD):

Develop a comprehensive GDD outlining every aspect of your game.

Include details on gameplay mechanics, characters, story, art style, and audio.

3. Storyboarding and Flowcharts:

Use storyboards or flowcharts to visualize the flow of your game.

Map out user interactions, game levels, and any branching storylines.

Story and Characters:

4. Craft a Compelling Storyline:

Develop a captivating narrative that aligns with your game concept.

Consider character motivations, conflicts, and plot twists.

5. Character Design:

Create detailed character profiles, including visual designs and backstories.

Ensure characters complement the game's theme and narrative.

Gameplay Mechanics:

6. Define Core Mechanics:

Identify the fundamental gameplay mechanics that will define the player's experience.

Ensure these mechanics align with your game's genre and concept.

7. Prototyping:

Build prototypes to test and iterate on your gameplay mechanics.

Seek feedback and make adjustments to enhance player engagement.

Art and Aesthetics:

8. Art Style:

Choose an art style that complements your game concept.

Consider factors like color palette, visual consistency, and thematic elements.

9. Create Concept Art:

Develop concept art for key elements, such as characters, environments, and objects.

Use this art to guide the creation of final assets.

Sound and Music:

10. Sound Design:

Plan the audio elements that will enhance the gaming experience.

Consider ambient sounds, character voices, and sound effects.

11. Compose or Source Music:

Create a soundtrack or source music that fits the mood of your game.

Ensure music enhances the overall atmosphere and gameplay.

User Interface (UI) Design:

12. Design Intuitive UI:

Create a user-friendly interface that enhances the player's experience.

Consider the placement of buttons, menus, and other interactive elements.

13. User Testing:

Conduct user testing for the UI to identify any usability issues.

Iterate on the design based on feedback to improve user interaction.

Iterate and Refine:

14. Playtesting:

Regularly playtest your game to identify potential issues and gather player feedback.

Use this feedback to refine gameplay mechanics, address bugs, and enhance overall player satisfaction.

15.Iterate on Design:

Embrace an iterative design process. Be willing to make adjustments based on testing and feedback.

Continuously refine and polish your game design as you progress through development.

By investing time and thought into the design phase, you set the foundation for a cohesive and engaging gaming experience.

Remember to remain flexible, embrace creativity, and be open to refining your design as your game takes shape.

# 4

# Create Game Assets

4. Create Game Assets:

Creating game assets involves developing the visual and auditory elements that bring your game to life. Here's a comprehensive guide to help you navigate the process:

Graphics and Visual Assets:

1. Understand Art Requirements:

Identify the visual style and requirements of your game.

Determine if you need 2D or 3D assets based on your chosen game development platform.

2. Graphic Design Tools:

Utilize graphic design software like Adobe Photoshop, Illustrator, or free alternatives like GIMP and Inkscape.

Learn the basics of creating and editing images, textures, and sprites.

3. Character Design:

Develop detailed character designs based on your game's narrative and style.

Create character sheets illustrating various poses and expressions.

4. Environment and Level Design:

Design environments and levels to match your game's theme.

Create assets such as backgrounds, platforms, and decorative elements.

5. Asset Optimization:

Optimize assets for performance by considering file sizes and resolutions.

Use compression techniques without compromising visual quality.

3D Modeling and Animation:

6. Choose 3D Modeling Software:

If working in 3D, choose software like Blender, Autodesk Maya, or Cinema 4D.

Learn the basics of modeling, texturing, and animating 3D objects.

7. Character Rigging and Animation:

If your game involves 3D characters, understand rigging for skeletal animation.

Animate characters using keyframes to bring them to life.

8. Environmental Assets:

Model 3D environments and props to populate your game world.

Consider lighting and shading for a visually appealing atmosphere.

Sound and Music:

9. Sound Effects:

Create or source sound effects that match in-game actions.

Pay attention to details like footsteps, interactions, and ambient sounds.

10.Music Composition:

Compose original music or license music that fits your game's mood.

Ensure that the music enhances the overall gaming experience.

UI and Interactive Elements:

11. Design UI Elements:

Create visually appealing buttons, icons, and menus for your game's user interface.

Ensure consistency in design to provide a cohesive user experience.

12. Animated UI Elements:

If applicable, add animations to UI elements to make interactions more engaging.

Use subtle animations to guide the player's attention.

Collaboration and Resources:

13. Asset Libraries:

Explore asset libraries and marketplaces for pre-made assets, especially if time or resources are limited.

Ensure compatibility with your chosen game development platform.

14. Collaborate with Artists and Musicians:

If you're not a designer or musician, consider collaborating with professionals.

Platforms like ArtStation, Behance, and SoundCloud can help you find collaborators.

Testing and Iteration:

15. Test Asset Integration:

Integrate assets into your game environment and test their functionality.

Ensure that assets align with your original design and enhance the overall gaming experience.

16.Iterate Based on Feedback:

Gather feedback from playtesting and adjust assets accordingly.

Iterate on design elements to improve visual and auditory aspects of your game.

By carefully crafting your game assets, you contribute significantly to the overall quality and immersion of your game.

31

Remember to maintain a consistent visual and auditory style throughout your project and be open to refining your assets as your game progresses.

# 5

# Game Development

5. Game Development:

Now that you have your game design and assets in place, it's time to dive into the development process. Let's explore the key steps and considerations for building your game:

Programming and Coding:

1. Understand the Basics of Your Chosen Platform:

Revisit the basics of your chosen game development platform (Unity, Unreal Engine, Godot).

Familiarize yourself with the platform's coding language (C#, C++, GDScript).

2. Set Up Your Development Environment:

Install the necessary software, including the game engine and any plugins or extensions you might need.

Configure your integrated development environment (IDE) for a smooth workflow.

3. Create a Project Structure:

Organize your project with a clear folder structure.

Categorize assets, scripts, and other resources logically for easy navigation.

4. Game Architecture:

Plan the architecture of your game, considering the relationships between different game elements.

Implement modular and scalable code for easier maintenance.

Implementing Game Mechanics:

5. Start with Core Mechanics:

Begin by implementing the core gameplay mechanics outlined in your game design document.

Test these mechanics to ensure they work as intended.

6. Player Controls:

Implement responsive and intuitive controls for player interaction.

Consider touch controls for mobile games or joystick support for console games.

7. AI Development:

If your game involves non-player characters (NPCs), design and implement AI behaviors.

Balance AI difficulty levels to provide an engaging experience.

Level Design and Environment:

8. Build Game Levels:

Create the levels based on your level design from the game design document.

Implement progression and challenges to maintain player engagement.

9.Environmental Interactivity:

Add interactive elements to the environment, such as switches, doors, or destructible objects.

Ensure that the environment contributes to the overall narrative and gameplay.

Audio Integration:

10. Integrate Sound Effects:

Implement sound effects in response to in-game actions.

Use audio cues to enhance the player's understanding of the game world.

11. Implement Music:

Integrate your composed or sourced music into the game.

Consider dynamic music systems that adapt to the gameplay situation.

Testing and Debugging:

12. Regular Playtesting:

Conduct frequent playtests to identify bugs, glitches, or gameplay issues.

Gather feedback from playtesters to refine and improve the gaming experience.

13. Debugging:

Use debugging tools provided by your game development platform.

Address any issues promptly to maintain a stable game environment.

Optimization and Performance:

14. Optimize for Performance:

Optimize game assets and code for better performance.

Consider mobile devices' limitations and ensure your game runs smoothly.

15.Cross-Platform Considerations:

If targeting multiple platforms, test and optimize for each one individually.

Ensure consistent performance across various devices.

Version Control and Collaboration:

16. Use Version Control Systems:

Implement version control systems like Git to track changes and collaborate effectively.

Regularly commit your code to maintain a history of changes.

17. Collaborate with Team Members:

If working in a team, communicate regularly and coordinate efforts.

Share progress, address challenges, and celebrate milestones together.

Documentation:

18. Document Your Code:

Comment your code thoroughly for future reference and collaboration.

Create documentation for other developers who may work on the project.

19. Create User Guides:

Develop user guides for players, explaining game mechanics and controls.

Ensure that players have the information they need for an enjoyable experience.

Continuous Improvement:

20. Iterate and Update:

Gather feedback from playtesting, reviews, and player engagement.

Iterate on your game by releasing updates that address issues and introduce new features.

Remember that game development is an iterative process.

Stay adaptable, be open to feedback, and enjoy the creative journey as your game evolves from concept to a fully realized experience.

# 6

# Optimize for Mobile

6. Optimize for Mobile:

Optimizing your game for mobile platforms is crucial to ensure a smooth and enjoyable user experience. Here's a comprehensive guide on how to optimize your game for mobile devices:

Understand Mobile Constraints:

1. Performance Considerations:

Mobile devices have varied hardware capabilities. Consider performance constraints and optimize your game accordingly.

Test your game on a range of devices to ensure compatibility.

2. Screen Sizes and Resolutions:

Account for different screen sizes and resolutions.

Use responsive design principles to adapt your game's interface to various devices.

Mobile-Friendly Controls:

3.Touch Controls:

Design intuitive touch controls for mobile gameplay.

Ensure buttons are appropriately sized and spaced for easy interaction.

4.Gesture Support:

Consider integrating gestures, such as swiping and pinching, for more immersive controls.

Provide clear instructions or tutorials for new players.

Asset Optimization:

5. Texture Compression:

Compress textures to reduce the size of image assets.

Use texture atlases to optimize rendering and minimize draw calls.

6. Model and Animation Complexity:

Optimize 3D models and animations for mobile performance.

Use LODs (Level of Detail) for 3D models to adjust detail based on distance.

Battery and Resource Management:

7. Energy Efficiency:

Implement energy-efficient coding practices to minimize battery consumption.

Avoid continuous background processes that drain battery life.

8. Memory Management:

Optimize memory usage to prevent crashes on devices with limited RAM.

Unload unused assets and resources during gameplay.

Network and Connectivity:

9.Offline Play:

Provide offline play options to accommodate users in areas with limited connectivity.

Implement mechanisms to sync data when the device reconnects.

10. Data Usage:

Minimize data usage, especially for online features.

Compress data when transmitting information between the game and servers.

User Interface (UI) Adaptation:

11.Responsive UI:

Ensure your game's UI adapts to different screen sizes.

Test UI elements on various devices to verify readability and usability.

12.Text Size and Readability:

Adjust text size for mobile screens to ensure readability.

Use legible fonts and consider localization requirements.

Platform-Specific Features:

13. Utilize Mobile Features:

Take advantage of mobile device features such as gyroscopes, accelerometers, and touch gestures to enhance gameplay.

Consider implementing features like push notifications for engagement.

14.App Permissions:

Request app permissions only when necessary to build user trust.

Clearly communicate why certain permissions are required.

Testing on Real Devices:

15. Device Testing:

Test your game on a variety of real devices to identify platform-specific issues.

Use emulators for initial testing but prioritize real devices for accurate results.

16. User Feedback:

Gather feedback from beta testers and early users on mobile-specific challenges.

Address reported issues promptly to enhance the mobile experience.

Store Optimization:

17.App Store Guidelines:

Familiarize yourself with the guidelines of the app store you're targeting (e.g., Google Play Store, Apple App Store).

Ensure your game complies with submission requirements.

18. App Store Optimization (ASO):

Optimize your app store listing with relevant keywords and compelling visuals.

Monitor and respond to user reviews to address concerns and improve ratings.

Continuous Improvement:

19. Analytics:

Implement analytics to track user behavior and identify areas for improvement.

Use analytics data to make informed decisions for future updates.

20. Regular Updates:

Release regular updates to address performance issues, add new features, and enhance the overall gaming experience.

Keep the game content fresh to retain user interest.

Optimizing for mobile is an ongoing process that involves attention to detail and a commitment to delivering a seamless experience across a diverse range of devices.

Stay attuned to user feedback and technological advancements to continuously refine and enhance your mobile game.

# 7

# Monetization Strategy

7. Monetization Strategy:

Developing a successful monetization strategy for your game involves thoughtful planning and consideration of various models. Here's a comprehensive guide to help you create an effective approach:

Understand Monetization Models:

1.Free-to-Play (F2P):

Offer your game for free and generate revenue through in-app purchases, advertisements, or other optional purchases.

Consider offering a compelling in-app purchase system that enhances the gaming experience without creating paywalls.

2.Freemium:

Provide a basic version of your game for free and offer premium features or content as in-app purchases.

Ensure that the free version is engaging enough to attract a wide user base.

3.Paid Game:

Charge an upfront fee for users to download and access your game.

This model works best for games with a strong reputation, unique content, or a niche target audience.

In-App Purchases (IAPs):

4. Virtual Goods:

Integrate virtual goods that players can purchase, such as cosmetic items, power-ups, or in-game currency.

Ensure these items enhance the gaming experience without creating an imbalance.

5. Consumable vs. Non-Consumable Purchases:

Differentiate between consumable items (e.g., in-game currency) and non-consumable items (e.g., permanent power-ups).

Clearly communicate the value of each type of purchase to users.

Advertisement Integration:

6.Ad-Based Revenue:

Implement ads strategically to generate revenue.

Offer ad-free options for users who make in-app purchases or subscribe to premium features.

7.Ad Formats:

Explore various ad formats, including banner ads, interstitial ads, and rewarded video ads.

Opt for non-intrusive ad placements to maintain a positive user experience.

Subscription Models:

8. Subscription Tiers:

Offer different subscription tiers with varying benefits.

Provide exclusive content, early access, or premium features to subscribers.

9.Trial Periods:

Implement trial periods for subscriptions to allow users to experience premium features before committing.

Clearly communicate the value of the subscription to encourage conversions.

Strategic Pricing:

10.Competitive Pricing:

Research competitors' pricing models within your game genre.

Price your in-app purchases or premium game access competitively.

11. Localized Pricing:

Consider regional pricing to accommodate users in different countries.

Adjust prices based on the economic conditions of target markets.

User Engagement and Retention:

12. Engaging Content Updates:

Regularly release new content, features, or events to keep players engaged.

Use updates to promote in-app purchases and subscriptions.

13. Rewards and Loyalty Programs:

Implement rewards for loyal players, encouraging continuous engagement.

Offer discounts, exclusive items, or in-game currency as part of loyalty programs.

Analytics and Data-Driven Decisions:

14.Implement Analytics Tools:

Integrate analytics tools to track user behavior, conversion rates, and revenue sources.

Use data to make informed decisions about your monetization strategy.

15. A/B Testing:

Conduct A/B testing on different pricing models, ad placements, or in-app purchase offerings.

Optimize your strategy based on the results of these tests.

User Communication:

16. Transparent Communication:

Clearly communicate your monetization strategy to users.

Provide transparency about how in-app purchases or ads contribute to the game's development.

17. User Feedback Channels:

Establish channels for user feedback regarding monetization.

Listen to user concerns and address them promptly to build trust.

Legal and Ethical Considerations:

18. Compliance with App Store Policies:

Ensure your monetization strategy complies with the policies of the app store you're using (e.g., Google Play Store, Apple App Store).

Stay informed about policy updates.

19. Ethical Monetization:

Prioritize user experience and avoid manipulative or aggressive monetization tactics.

Build a positive reputation by treating users fairly.

Continuous Optimization:

20. Iterative Improvement:

Continuously evaluate the performance of your monetization strategy.

Iterate based on user feedback, industry trends, and changes in your game's lifecycle.

Creating a successful monetization strategy requires a balance between generating revenue and providing value to players.


By understanding your target audience, staying adaptable, and continuously optimizing your approach, you can create a sustainable and user-friendly monetization model for your game.

# 8

# Set Up a Developer Account

8. Set Up a Developer Account:

Creating a developer account is a crucial step in bringing your game to the Google Play Store. Here's an extensive guide to help you navigate the process:

1. Research Developer Account Requirements:

Google Play Console: Understand the features and requirements of the Google Play Console, the platform for managing your apps on the Play Store.

Developer Policies: Familiarize yourself with Google Play's Developer Program Policies. Ensure your app complies with these policies to prevent issues during the review process.

2. Prepare Necessary Information:

Legal Entity Information: If you're publishing as a company or organization, have your legal entity details ready, including business name, address, and tax information.

Payment Details: Set up a Google Payments Merchant account and have your banking information ready for receiving payments.

Developer Profile: Create a concise and engaging developer profile, which will be visible on the Play Store.

3. Create a Google Account:

Google Account: If you don't already have one, create a Google Account. This will be used to access the Google Play Console.

Two-Factor Authentication: Enable two-factor authentication for added security.

4. Access the Google Play Console:

Console Access: Go to the [Google Play Console](https://play.google.com/console) and sign in with your Google Account.

Developer Agreement: Review and accept the Developer Distribution Agreement, which outlines the terms for distributing apps on the Play Store.

5. Set Up Your Developer Profile:

Developer Name: Choose a developer name that aligns with your brand or game identity. This name will be displayed on the Play Store.

Profile Details: Complete your developer profile with relevant information, including contact details and a profile image.

6. Enroll as a Developer:

Payment Setup: Set up your payment details. Google requires a one-time registration fee, and you need to provide valid banking information for payouts.

Enrollment: Complete the developer enrollment process by paying the registration fee. This step may take a few hours to a day for processing.

7. Understand the Google Play Console Dashboard:

Dashboard Overview: Familiarize yourself with the Google Play Console dashboard. This is where you'll manage your apps, track performance, and access various tools.

Sections and Tabs: Explore different sections such as "Dashboard," "Release," "Store Presence," and "Statistics" to understand the console's functionalities.

8. Set Up App Listings:

Create a New App: Start by creating a new app listing for your game. Provide essential information such as the title, description, and screenshots.

Graphics and Multimedia:Upload high-quality graphics, including the app icon, feature graphic, and promotional images.

Categorization: Choose relevant categories and tags to help users discover your game.

9. Implement Monetization:

Pricing and Distribution: Set the pricing model for your game – whether it's free, paid, or includes in-app purchases.

Determine the countries or regions where your app will be available.

Monetization Strategies: If your game includes in-app purchases or advertisements, configure the necessary settings in the console.

10. Testing and Publishing:

Alpha and Beta Testing: Utilize the alpha and beta testing features to gather feedback and identify potential issues before the official release.

Submit for Review: When you're confident in your game's readiness, submit it for review. Google's review process ensures apps meet quality and policy standards.

11. Stay Informed:

Policy Updates: Regularly check for updates to Google Play's policies. Staying informed helps you adapt your game to any policy changes.

Developer Resources: Explore additional resources provided by Google, including documentation, blog posts, and community forums, to enhance your understanding of the platform.

12. Monitor and Iterate:

User Feedback: Pay attention to user reviews and feedback on the Play Store. Address issues promptly and use feedback to make improvements.

Analytics: Utilize the analytics tools in the Google Play Console to track user engagement, downloads, and other performance metrics.

Setting up a developer account on the Google Play Console is a significant milestone in bringing your game to a global audience.

By following these steps and staying engaged with the developer community, you set the stage for a successful and well-managed presence on the Play Store.

# 9

# Implement User Feedback System

9. Implement User Feedback System:

Implementing a robust user feedback system is crucial for understanding your players, identifying issues, and continuously improving your game. Here's an extensive guide on setting up an effective user feedback system:

1. In-Game Feedback Mechanism:

Feedback Button: Integrate a visible feedback button within your game's interface.

User Prompts: Prompt users to provide feedback after specific in-game events or milestones.

2. External Feedback Platforms:

Review Platforms: Encourage users to leave reviews on app stores (e.g., Google Play Store, Apple App Store).

Social Media: Leverage social media platforms for discussions and feedback

Community Forums: Create or participate in forums where players can share their thoughts.

3. Surveys and Questionnaires:

In-Game Surveys: Implement occasional in-game surveys to gather specific information from players.

Email Surveys: Send surveys via email to collect detailed feedback from players who have opted in.

4. User Ratings and Reviews:

Monitor Ratings: Regularly monitor user ratings on app stores. Positive and negative reviews provide valuable insights.

Respond to Reviews: Engage with users by responding to reviews. Acknowledge feedback and communicate any updates or fixes.

5. Analytics and Player Behavior:

Analytics Tools: Utilize analytics tools to track player behavior within the game.

Identify Patterns: Look for patterns in player actions and use this data to address common pain points.

6. Community Engagement:

Official Community Channels: Create official community channels, such as forums or social media groups, where players can discuss the game.

Moderation: Appoint moderators to manage community discussions and report valuable insights.

7. Customer Support:

Responsive Support: Establish responsive customer support channels for direct communication with players.

FAQs and Knowledge Base: Create a comprehensive FAQ section or knowledge base to address common queries.

8. Beta Testing and Early Access:

Beta Test Programs: Conduct beta testing before a full release to gather feedback from a diverse group of players.

Early Access Models: If applicable, consider early access models that involve the community in the development process.

9. Feedback Categories:

Bug Reports: Encourage users to report bugs with detailed descriptions of the issue and the steps to reproduce.

Feature Requests: Create a space for players to suggest new features or improvements.

General Feedback: Provide an option for general comments and feedback about the overall gaming experience.

10. Regular Surveys:

Scheduled Surveys: Implement periodic surveys to gauge long-term satisfaction and preferences.

Incentivize Participation: Consider providing incentives for completing surveys, such as in-game rewards.

11. Privacy and Anonymity:

Anonymous Feedback: Allow users to submit feedback anonymously if they prefer.

Privacy Policies: Clearly communicate how user data will be used and ensure compliance with privacy policies.

12. Iterate Based on Feedback:

Feedback Analysis: Regularly analyze collected feedback to identify trends and prioritize areas for improvement.

Iterative Development: Implement changes and updates based on user feedback, demonstrating a commitment to continuous improvement.

13. Version Release Notes:

Communicate Changes: In your version release notes, communicate how feedback has influenced updates.

Show Appreciation: Acknowledge and thank the community for their contributions.

14. User Recognition:

Feature User Contributions: Highlight exceptional feedback or contributions from users in the game.

In-Game Credits: Consider including a section in the game credits to recognize valuable feedback.

15. Monitoring Social Media:

Social Listening Tools: Use social listening tools to monitor mentions of your game on social media.

Engage Actively: Engage in conversations, respond to queries, and address concerns raised on social platforms.

Implementing a comprehensive user feedback system not only helps in resolving issues but also fosters a sense of community around your game. By actively listening to your players, you create a collaborative environment that contributes to the ongoing success of your game.

# 10

# Develop a Marketing Strategy

10. Develop a Marketing Strategy:

Creating a robust marketing strategy is essential to make your game stand out in the competitive landscape. Here's an extensive guide to help you develop an effective marketing plan:

1. Define Your Target Audience:

Demographics: Identify the age, gender, location, and interests of your target audience.

Player Persona: Create a player persona to understand the motivations and preferences of your ideal players.

2. Build a Strong Brand:

Game Identity: Develop a unique and memorable identity for your game.

Logo and Visuals: Design a recognizable logo and visuals that represent the theme and tone of your game.

3. Create a Compelling Game Trailer:

Highlight Key Features: Showcase the most exciting and unique aspects of your game.

Engaging Narrative: Craft a compelling narrative that captivates viewers.

Professional Quality: Ensure high production values and professional editing.

4. Establish an Online Presence:

Website: Create a dedicated website for your game with essential information, screenshots, and a download link.

Social Media Profiles: Utilize platforms like Twitter, Facebook, Instagram, and TikTok to engage with your audience.

5. Leverage Social Media Marketing:

Consistent Posting: Regularly share updates, behind-the-scenes content, and engaging posts.

Visual Content: Use eye-catching visuals, GIFs, and short videos to grab attention.

Community Engagement: Foster a sense of community by responding to comments and interacting with your audience.

6. Influencer Marketing:

Identify Influencers: Identify influencers or content creators in the gaming industry.

Collaborate: Reach out for collaboration to have your game featured in their content.

Reviews and Let's Plays: Encourage influencers to create reviews or let's play videos.

7. Utilize Game Development Forums:

Indie Game Communities: Participate in indie game forums and communities to share updates and seek feedback.

Developer Platforms: Utilize platforms like itch.io and Game Jolt to showcase your game to a dedicated audience.

8. Content Marketing:

Dev Blogs: Start a development blog to document the journey of creating your game.

Guest Posts: Contribute guest posts to relevant gaming blogs or websites to reach a wider audience.

9. Email Marketing:

Build a Subscriber List: Encourage players to subscribe to your newsletter for updates.

Newsletter Campaigns: Send regular newsletters with exclusive content, announcements, and special offers.

10. Pre-Launch Campaigns:

Teasers and Countdowns: Build anticipation with teaser trailers and countdowns to launch.

Demo Releases: Release playable demos or beta versions to generate excitement.

## 11. Cross-Promotion:

Collaborate with Other Developers: Explore cross-promotion opportunities with other indie developers.

Shared Audiences: Identify games with a similar target audience for effective cross-promotion.

## 12. App Store Optimization (ASO):

Keyword Optimization: Use relevant keywords in your app's title and description for improved discoverability.

Eye-Catching Screenshots: Showcase engaging screenshots that highlight key aspects of your game.

## 13. Public Relations (PR):

Press Releases: Create press releases for significant announcements or milestones.

Media Kit: Develop a media kit with high-resolution images, press releases, and key information for journalists.

14. Community Engagement Events:

Livestreams and Q&A Sessions: Host live events to interact with your audience, answer questions, and showcase gameplay.

Contests and Giveaways: Run contests or giveaways to encourage participation and increase visibility.

15. Post-Launch Marketing:

Update Announcements: Share regular updates about new features, bug fixes, and content additions.

Player Stories: Highlight positive player experiences and testimonials to build trust.

16. Analytics and Iteration:

Track Performance: Use analytics tools to monitor the performance of your marketing efforts.

Iterate Strategies: Based on data, iterate and refine your marketing strategies for ongoing improvement.

17. Budget Allocation:

Allocate Marketing Budget: Allocate a portion of your budget specifically for marketing efforts.

Paid Advertising: Consider targeted paid advertising on social media platforms or gaming websites.

18. Partnerships and Collaborations:

Strategic Partnerships: Explore partnerships with relevant brands or organizations.

Coordinated Launches: Coordinate launches with gaming events or industry milestones for added visibility.

19. Reviews and Influencer Feedback:

Monitor Reviews: Regularly monitor user reviews on app stores and address concerns promptly.

Feedback Utilization: Use player feedback, positive or negative, to inform future updates and marketing strategies.

20. Adaptability and Continuous Improvement:

Stay Adaptive: Be flexible and adapt your marketing strategy based on changing trends and player preferences.

Learn from Data: Continuously learn from analytics data and player behavior to refine and optimize your approach.

Developing a successful marketing strategy requires a combination of creativity, consistency, and adaptability.

By implementing these strategies and staying engaged with your audience, you can effectively promote your game and build a dedicated player community.

# 11

# Implementing In-App Purchases (IAPs)

11. Implementing In-App Purchases (IAPs):

In-app purchases (IAPs) can be a significant revenue stream for your game, but their successful implementation requires careful planning and consideration.

Here's an extensive guide on how to effectively integrate in-app purchases into your game:

1. Understand In-App Purchase Models:

Consumable Purchases: Items that can be used or consumed, like in-game currency or power-ups.

Non-Consumable Purchases: Permanent items, such as additional levels or features.

Subscription Models: Recurring payments for access to premium features or content.

2. Define Your Monetization Strategy:

Balanced Approach: Strike a balance between generating revenue and providing value to players.

Player Experience: Ensure that in-app purchases enhance the player experience without creating a pay-to-win environment.

3. Plan Your Virtual Economy:

In-Game Currency: If applicable, design an in-game currency system.

Economy Balance: Determine the earning rate and scarcity of in-game currency to maintain a balanced virtual economy.

4. Offer Diverse In-App Purchases:

Virtual Goods: Create a variety of virtual goods, such as cosmetic items, customization options, or unique characters.

Power-Ups and Boosts: Develop power-ups or boosts that enhance gameplay without compromising balance.

5. Optimize Pricing and Value:

Competitive Pricing: Research competitors and set competitive prices for your in-app purchases.

Perceived Value: Clearly communicate the value of each purchase to users.

6. Implement Secure Payment Systems:

Secure Transactions: Utilize secure payment gateways to protect user financial information.

User Trust: Build trust by ensuring a transparent and secure payment process.

7. Provide Limited-Time Offers:

Special Deals: Introduce limited-time offers, discounts, or bundles to encourage purchases.

Seasonal Events: Align promotions with seasonal events or updates to boost engagement.

8. Implement In-App Purchase UI:

Intuitive Interface: Design an intuitive and user-friendly interface for making in-app purchases.

Clear Descriptions: Clearly describe what each purchase offers, including any bonuses or discounts.

9. Reward-Based In-App Purchases:

Achievement Rewards: Offer in-app purchases as rewards for completing achievements.

Progression Bonuses: Provide discounts or exclusive items for players who reach certain milestones.

10. Subscription Models:

Tiered Subscriptions: If using a subscription model, offer different tiers with varying benefits.

Trial Periods: Allow users to experience premium features with trial periods before committing.

11. Implement Consumable Purchases:

Balanced Use: Ensure consumable purchases do not unbalance the gameplay.

Regular Consumption: Encourage regular use to maintain engagement.

12. Provide Non-Intrusive Ads:

Ad-Based Revenue: If using ads, ensure they are non-intrusive and provide an opt-out option for in-app purchases.

Reward Videos: Implement rewarded video ads to offer in-game rewards for watching ads.

13. Test and Iterate:

A/B Testing: Conduct A/B testing on pricing, offers, and in-app purchase placements.

Iterate Based on Data: Use analytics data and user feedback to iterate on your in-app purchase strategy.

14. Consider In-App Purchase Events:

Special Events: Introduce in-app purchase events tied to in-game events or updates.

Limited Edition Items: Offer limited edition or exclusive items during events to drive sales.

15. Promote In-App Purchases Effectively:

In-Game Promotion: Strategically promote in-app purchases within the game interface.

Social Media Promotion: Leverage social media to highlight special offers and exclusive items.

16. In-App Purchase Analytics:

Track Conversion Rates: Use analytics to track how many users make purchases after viewing in-app purchase options.

Understand Player Behavior: Analyze player behavior to refine your in-app purchase strategy.

17. Support User Loyalty Programs:

Loyalty Rewards: Implement loyalty programs that reward users for consistent in-app purchases.

Exclusive Benefits: Offer exclusive benefits to users who frequently engage with in-app purchases.

18. Legal Compliance:

App Store Guidelines: Ensure that your in-app purchases comply with the guidelines of the app store you're using.

Transparency: Clearly communicate pricing, terms, and conditions to users.

19. Regularly Update In-App Purchases:

Refresh Offerings: Regularly update your in-app purchase options to keep content fresh.

Seasonal Content: Introduce seasonal or themed in-app purchases to coincide with events or holidays.

20. Community Engagement:

Communicate Changes: Communicate changes or additions to in-app purchases through community channels.

Gather Feedback: Solicit feedback from the community regarding in-app purchases to address concerns.

Effectively implementing in-app purchases requires a thoughtful and player-centric approach.

By providing value, maintaining balance, and actively engaging with your player community, you can create a successful in-app purchase system that enhances both player experience and revenue generation.

# 12

# Implement Effective User Onboarding

12. Implement Effective User Onboarding:

User onboarding is a critical aspect of ensuring that players have a positive and engaging experience from the moment they launch your game. Here's an extensive guide on how to implement effective user onboarding:

1. Understand Your Audience:

Player Personas:Create player personas to understand the preferences and expectations of your target audience.

User Demographics: Consider the age, gaming experience, and preferences of your users.

2. Develop a Clear Onboarding Flow:

Simplicity is Key: Keep the onboarding process simple and straightforward.

Step-by-Step Guidance: Introduce game mechanics and features gradually through step-by-step guidance.

3. Provide a Guided Tutorial:

Interactive Tutorial: Develop an interactive tutorial that allows players to learn by doing.

Clear Instructions: Provide clear and concise instructions for each game mechanic.

4. Engaging Story or Theme:

Narrative Introduction: Introduce players to the game's world or story during onboarding.

Immersive Experience: Make onboarding an immersive part of the overall game experience.

5. Introduce Core Mechanics:

Focus on Basics: Prioritize introducing core game mechanics that are fundamental to gameplay.

Hands-On Learning: Allow players to practice basic actions during the onboarding phase.

6. Interactive Elements:

Clickable Elements: Include interactive elements in the onboarding process to encourage engagement.

Feedback Mechanisms: Provide immediate feedback for actions taken during onboarding.

7. Personalize the Experience:

Player Customization: If applicable, allow players to customize their characters or settings during onboarding.

Adaptive Learning: Personalize the onboarding experience based on player choices or preferences.

8. Showcase Progression Path:

Visual Progression: Display the player's progress through the onboarding process visually.

Rewards for Completion: Provide small rewards or acknowledgments for completing onboarding steps.

9. Utilize Gamification Elements:

Achievements: Introduce simple achievements or badges during onboarding.

Mini-Games: Incorporate mini-games or challenges that align with learning objectives.

10. Incentivize Learning:

Reward System: Implement a reward system for successfully completing onboarding.

In-Game Currency: Offer in-game currency or items as incentives for progressing through onboarding.

11. Mobile-Friendly Design:

Touch Controls: If designing for mobile, ensure onboarding is optimized for touch controls.

Responsive UI: Create a responsive user interface that adapts to various screen sizes.

12. Clear Calls-to-Action:

Highlight Actions: Clearly highlight the actions players need to take during onboarding.

Intuitive Navigation: Ensure players can easily navigate through onboarding screens.

13. Provide Help and Support:

FAQs and Help Section: Include a help section or FAQs within the game for quick reference.

Customer Support Access: Provide access to customer support during onboarding in case players encounter issues.

14. Test with Real Users:

Beta Testing: Conduct beta testing with real users to gather feedback on the onboarding experience.

Usability Testing: Test the onboarding flow for usability and make adjustments based on user feedback.

15. Iterate Based on Feedback:

Continuous Improvement: Use player feedback and analytics to iterate and improve the onboarding process.

Address Pain Points:Identify and address any pain points or confusion reported by users.

16. Cross-Platform Consistency:

Consistent Experience: Ensure a consistent onboarding experience across different platforms.

Unified Progression: If players switch devices, their onboarding progress should be seamlessly carried over.

17. Monitor Drop-off Points:

Analytics Tracking: Use analytics tools to monitor drop-off points during onboarding.

Optimize Problematic Areas: Identify and optimize areas where players commonly disengage.

18. Accessibility Considerations:

Accessibility Features: Implement accessibility features to cater to players with different needs.

Clear Text and Icons: Ensure that text and icons are clear and easily readable.

19. Encourage Social Connectivity:

Social Integration: If applicable, introduce social features during onboarding.

Friend Invitations: Encourage players to connect with friends or invite them to the game.

20. Onboarding Analytics:

User Behavior Tracking: Implement analytics to track user behavior during onboarding.

Conversion Rates: Analyze conversion rates from onboarding to regular gameplay.

Implementing effective user onboarding is an ongoing process that requires a balance between providing information and maintaining player engagement.

By focusing on user needs, gathering feedback, and continuously refining the onboarding experience, you can ensure that players start your game with a positive and enjoyable introduction.

# 13

# Optimize Game Performance

13. Optimize Game Performance:

Ensuring optimal performance is crucial for a positive gaming experience and player retention. Here's an extensive guide on how to effectively optimize your game's performance:

1. Performance Metrics:

FPS (Frames Per Second): Aim for a stable and high frame rate to provide smooth gameplay.

Latency: Minimize input lag and optimize network latency for responsive controls.

Memory Usage: Keep memory usage efficient to prevent crashes and slowdowns.

2. Cross-Platform Optimization:

Device Compatibility: Optimize your game to run smoothly on a variety of devices.

Screen Resolutions: Adapt your game's resolution to different screen sizes without sacrificing quality.

3. Graphics Settings:

Quality Levels: Implement adjustable graphics settings (low, medium, high) for users to customize based on their device capabilities.

Shader Complexity: Optimize shaders and graphics effects for better performance on lower-end devices.

4. Asset Compression:

Texture Compression: Use efficient texture compression techniques to reduce file sizes.

Model Simplification: Simplify 3D models without compromising visual quality.

5. Loading Times:

Asynchronous Loading: Implement asynchronous loading to prevent long wait times during startup.

Progress Indicators: Provide visual cues to inform players about loading progress.

6. Code Optimization:

Efficient Algorithms: Use efficient algorithms and data structures to improve processing speed.

Code Profiling: Use profiling tools to identify and optimize performance bottlenecks.

7. Resource Management:

Object Pooling: Utilize object pooling for frequently instantiated game objects to reduce memory overhead.

Resource Unloading: Unload unnecessary assets to free up memory during gameplay.

8. Network Optimization:

Minimize Requests: Minimize the number of network requests to reduce latency.

Data Compression: Compress data sent over the network to optimize bandwidth usage.

9. Battery Efficiency:

Optimize Rendering: Implement techniques like occlusion culling to reduce unnecessary rendering and conserve device battery.

Background Processes: Minimize resource usage when the game is in the background.

10. UI Performance:

UI Batching: Batch UI elements to reduce draw calls and enhance performance.

Optimized Animations: Use efficient animation techniques for UI elements.

11. Audio Optimization:

Audio Streaming: Stream audio dynamically to reduce memory usage.

Sound Pooling: Use sound pooling to efficiently manage and reuse audio resources.

12. Testing Across Devices:

Device Testing Matrix: Test your game on a variety of devices to identify and address performance disparities.

Beta Testing: Conduct beta testing with users on different devices to gather performance feedback.

13. Continuous Monitoring:

Performance Analytics: Implement performance analytics to monitor FPS, memory usage, and other key metrics.

Error Tracking: Use error tracking tools to identify and resolve performance-related issues reported by users.

14. Regular Updates:

Performance Patches: Release regular updates with performance optimizations based on user feedback.

Compatibility Checks: Ensure ongoing compatibility with the latest devices and operating system updates.

15. Community Engagement:

Feedback Channels: Establish channels for users to report performance issues.

Acknowledgment: Acknowledge and communicate with the community regarding performance-related concerns.

16. Documentation:

Optimization Guides: Create documentation or guides for other developers contributing to the project, emphasizing performance best practices.

Asset Optimization Guidelines: Provide guidelines for artists and designers on creating optimized assets.

17. Platform-Specific Optimization:

Platform Guidelines: Follow platform-specific optimization guidelines provided by the operating system or hardware manufacturers.

API Optimization: Optimize the usage of platform-specific APIs for enhanced performance.

18. Benchmarking:

Benchmark Testing: Conduct benchmark testing to evaluate and compare your game's performance against industry standards.

Competitor Analysis: Analyze the performance of similar games to identify areas for improvement.

19. Load Balancing:

Server Load: Implement load balancing mechanisms for online multiplayer games.

Dynamic Scaling: Dynamically adjust server resources based on player activity.

20. Data-Driven Optimization:

Analytics-Informed Decisions: Utilize data from analytics tools to inform optimization decisions.

Iterative Improvement: Continuously iterate on performance improvements based on real-time data.

Optimizing game performance is an ongoing process that requires a combination of technical expertise, testing, and community collaboration.

By prioritizing performance optimization, you enhance the overall gaming experience, attract a wider audience, and contribute to the long-term success of your game.

# 14

# Implement Effective Monetization Strategies

14. Implement Effective Monetization Strategies:

Monetizing your game is a crucial aspect of sustaining development efforts and creating a viable business model. Here's an extensive guide on how to implement effective monetization strategies:

1. Diverse Monetization Models:

In-App Purchases (IAP): Offer virtual goods, power-ups, or other enhancements for real money.

Ads: Integrate ads, including banners, interstitials, or rewarded videos, to generate revenue.

Subscriptions: Provide subscription-based access to premium features, content, or services.

## 2. Player-Centric Approach:

Balanced Monetization: Prioritize a balance between revenue generation and providing value to players.

Avoid Pay-to-Win: Ensure that monetization does not create a pay-to-win environment, maintaining fair competition.

## 3. Freemium Model:

Free Access: Allow users to download and play the game for free.

In-App Purchases: Offer in-app purchases for additional content or features.

## 4 Ad Integration:

Strategic Placement: Integrate ads strategically without disrupting the gameplay experience.

Rewarded Ads: Implement rewarded video ads to offer in-game rewards for user engagement.

5. In-App Purchase Strategy:

Virtual Goods: Create a variety of virtual goods, skins, or customization options.

Limited-Time Offers: Introduce limited-time offers, discounts, or bundles to encourage purchases.

6. Subscription Models:

Tiered Subscriptions: Offer different subscription tiers with varying benefits.

Free Trials: Provide free trial periods to entice users to subscribe.

7. Ad-Free Options:

Premium Version: Offer a premium version of the game without ads for a one-time purchase.

Ad Removal Purchase: Allow users to pay to remove ads from the free version.

8. Incentivized Monetization:

Daily Rewards: Implement daily rewards to encourage regular engagement.

Achievement Unlocks: Offer exclusive content or bonuses for completing in-game achievements.

9. Pricing Strategy:

Competitive Pricing: Research competitor pricing in your genre and set competitive prices.

Localization: Adjust prices based on regional considerations and currency exchange rates.

10. Seasonal Events and Sales:

Limited-Time Sales: Introduce seasonal events or sales with discounted in-app purchases.

Event-Specific Items: Offer exclusive items or content tied to special events.

11. Optimize Ad Revenue:

Ad Mediation: Use ad mediation platforms to maximize revenue from multiple ad networks.

Ad Placement Testing: Experiment with different ad placements to find the most effective locations.

12. In-Game Currency Systems:

Earnable Currency: Provide ways for players to earn in-game currency through gameplay.

Currency Bundles: Offer bundles of in-game currency at various price points.

13. Transparency and Trust:

Clear Pricing:Clearly communicate the pricing of in-app purchases and subscriptions.

Privacy Policies: Ensure compliance with privacy policies and communicate data usage practices transparently.

14. Monetization Analytics:

Track User Behavior: Use analytics tools to monitor how users engage with different monetization elements.

Conversion Rates: Analyze conversion rates for in-app purchases and ad clicks.

15. Player Feedback and Adaptation:

Listen to Users: Pay attention to player feedback on monetization aspects.

Iterative Improvement: Iterate on your monetization strategy based on user feedback and changing trends.

16. A/B Testing:

Experiment with Variations: Conduct A/B testing to experiment with different pricing models, ad placements, or in-app purchase offerings.

Data-Driven Decisions: Use data from A/B tests to make informed decisions on optimizing monetization elements.

17. Community Engagement:

Communication Channels: Establish communication channels to address player concerns or inquiries about monetization.

Community Polls: Use polls or surveys to gather player preferences on pricing or ad frequency.

18. Limited Interruption Ads:

Optimize Ad Frequency: Ensure that ads do not disrupt the gameplay experience with excessive interruptions.

Offer Opt-Outs: Provide options for users to reduce ad frequency through in-app purchases or rewarded video views.

19. Loyalty Programs:

Rewards for Loyal Players: Implement loyalty programs that offer exclusive benefits to long-time players.

Special Discounts: Provide discounts on in-app purchases or subscriptions for loyal users.

20. Ethical Monetization Practices:

Avoid Exploitative Tactics: Steer clear of manipulative or exploitative monetization practices.

User-Focused Value: Prioritize delivering value to users through your monetization strategies.

Implementing effective monetization strategies requires a delicate balance between generating revenue and maintaining a positive player experience.

By staying attentive to player feedback, adapting to industry trends, and continually refining your approach, you can create a sustainable and player-friendly monetization model for your game.

# 15

# Foster Community Engagement

15. Foster Community Engagement:

Building and nurturing a community around your game is essential for long-term success. Here's an extensive guide on how to effectively foster community engagement:

1. Establish Official Community Channels:

- Forums: Create official forums where players can discuss the game, share experiences, and connect.

-Social Media Groups: Set up dedicated groups on platforms like Facebook, Reddit, or Discord.

2. Active Community Moderation:

-Moderator Recruitment:Appoint active and passionate community members as moderators.

-Guidelines: Clearly communicate community guidelines and expectations.

3. Regular Developer Interaction:

-Developer Q&A Sessions: Host regular Q&A sessions where developers interact directly with the community.

-Announcement Updates: Keep the community informed about updates, upcoming features, and future plans.

4. In-Game Community Features:

- Player Profiles: Implement player profiles with achievements, statistics, and customization options.

- Clans or Guilds: Allow players to form in-game groups for collaboration and socialization.

5. Community Events:

- In-Game Events: Organize special in-game events, challenges, or tournaments.

-Real-World Gatherings: If feasible, host real-world gatherings or meetups for players.

6. User-Generated Content:

- Fan Art Contests: Encourage players to submit fan art or creations related to the game.

- Player Stories: Highlight player stories and experiences through social media or in-game features.

7. Engaging Content Creation:

- Encourage Streamers: Support and promote players who stream or create content related to your game.

- Content Creation Contests: Host contests for the best gameplay videos, guides, or creative content.

8. Official Communication Channels:

-Regular Updates: Provide regular updates through official channels, including social media, blogs, or newsletters.

- Community Spotlight: Shine a spotlight on notable community members or achievements.

9. Beta Testing and Feedback:

- Exclusive Beta Access: Offer exclusive beta testing opportunities to the community.

- Feedback Integration: Actively incorporate player feedback into the development process.

10. Community Feedback Surveys:

- Regular Surveys: Conduct surveys to gather feedback on specific aspects of the game or community.

- Incentivize Participation: Offer rewards or exclusive items for completing community surveys.

11. Community Challenges:

- Weekly or Monthly Challenges: Introduce challenges that encourage community participation and competition.

- Leaderboards: Display leaderboards for community challenges within the game.

12. Recognition and Rewards:

- Player of the Month: Highlight an outstanding community member each month.

-In-Game Recognition: Feature notable community members in the game's credits or with in-game titles.

13. Community Support Channels:

- Help Desk or Support Forum: Provide dedicated channels for players to seek assistance or report issues.

- Responsive Support Team: Ensure timely responses and resolutions from the support team.

14. Community Livestreams:

- Developer Livestreams: Host regular livestreams where developers showcase upcoming features or interact with the community.

- Player Livestreams: Encourage players to livestream their gameplay and interact with viewers.

15. Celebrate Milestones:

-Anniversary Events: Organize special events or giveaways to celebrate the game's anniversaries.

- Community Growth Milestones: Acknowledge and celebrate community growth milestones.

16. Community Guidelines:

- Positive Environment: Foster a positive and inclusive community environment.

- Anti-Toxicity Policies: Enforce anti-toxicity policies to maintain a welcoming space for all players.

17. Developer Blogs:

- Development Insights: Share behind-the-scenes insights into the game's development through developer blogs.

- Roadmaps: Provide roadmaps outlining future updates and features.

18. Exclusive Community Features:

- Beta Access: Offer exclusive access to beta versions or early builds for community members.

- Exclusive Items: Provide special in-game items or perks for dedicated community contributors.

19. Community Challenges:

- Weekly or Monthly Challenges: Introduce challenges that encourage community participation and competition.

-Leaderboards: Display leaderboards for community challenges within the game.

20. Cross-Promotions and Partnerships:

- Collaborate with Other Communities: Explore partnerships with communities related to gaming or shared interests.

-Cross-Promotions: Engage in cross-promotions with other game developers or content creators.

Building a vibrant and engaged community takes time and dedication.

By fostering a positive environment, actively communicating with your player base, and providing opportunities for player contribution, you can create a community that not only supports your game but becomes an integral part of its success.

www.ingramcontent.com/pod-product-compliance
Lightning Source LLC
Chambersburg PA
CBHW070852260726
48661CB00004B/1373